Protecting Habitats

Woodlands and Forests in Danger

Moira Butterfield

W
FRANKLIN WATTS
LONDON•SYDNEY

Designer Rita Storey
Editor Sarah Ridley
Art Director Jonathan Hair
Editor-in-Chief John C. Miles
Picture Research Susan Mennell
Map artwork Ian Thompson

© 2004 Franklin Watts

First published in 2004
by Franklin Watts
96 Leonard Street
London
EC2A 4XD

Franklin Watts Australia
45-51 Huntley Street
Alexandria
NSW 2015

ISBN 0 7496 5817 7

A CIP catalogue record for this book is
available from the British Library.

Printed in Hong Kong/China

Picture Credits
Cover images: Ecoscene

Ecoscene: pp.1, 4,7 ,8-9, 10, 11, 12, 16, 19,
20, 21, 22, 23, 24, 25, 26
Oxford Scientific Films: pp.15, 27

*Every attempt has been made to clear copyright.
Should there be any inadvertent omission, please
apply to the publisher for rectification.*

Note to parents and teachers

Every effort has been made by the Publishers to ensure that the
websites in this book are suitable for children, that they are of the
highest educational value, and that they contain no
inappropriate or offensive material. However, because of the
nature of the Internet, it is impossible to guarantee that the
contents of these sites will not be altered. We strongly advise that
Internet access is supervised by a responsible adult.

CONTENTS

All about forests

The densely packed trees of this Cornish woodland in late spring create a magical atmosphere as light filters through the green canopy.

Forests cover a vast area of our planet's surface. This huge environment is thought to have a significant effect on the Earth's weather, temperature and even the air we breathe.

Defining woodlands and forests

The Earth is divided by an imaginary line around its centre, called the equator. Above and below the equator lie the northern and southern hemispheres.

The more southerly part of the northern hemisphere is home to woodlands, made up mainly of deciduous trees that lose their leaves in winter. Further north there is the huge boreal forest, made up mainly of evergreen trees that keep their leaves the whole year round.

Many areas of Earth near the equator are wrapped in lush green tropical rainforests, which are not covered in this book. There are, however, areas of cooler, temperate rainforest in both the northern and southern hemisphere.

Standing among the trees

If you visited a woodland you would find a mixture of trees, such as maple, beech or birch. Many of them are broad-leaved trees. You might see birds and small mammals busy looking for food. On the ground you would find flowers growing on the forest floor. In winter, the trees would be bare and there would be a carpet of fallen leaves.

The boreal forest stretches around the world, through North America, Europe, Scandinavia and Asia. Two-thirds of it grow in Russia, where it is called the "taiga". Altogether it covers 16.6 million sq km (6.4 million sq miles), which makes it the largest land biome on Earth. Here you would be surrounded by trees such as firs, spruce and conifers. You would find less wildlife and fewer small plants.

If you stood in a temperate rainforest you would be surrounded by a small number of tree types, with some growing to a huge size. On the ground you would see mosses, ferns and other moisture-loving plants. It would be cool and wet most of the time.

BIOME UNDER THREAT

Forests have grown on Earth for hundreds of millions of years, and for centuries humans have cut them down for timber or to clear the land for farming. In modern times this process has speeded up. Another modern threat is industrial pollution. It has brought deadly acid rain to the forests, killing trees and poisoning the soil.

The loss of large forest areas is called "deforestation". In this book you can find out what is being done to control it, and how scientists are trying to battle the threat of pollution and predict what effect the loss of so many trees might have on the world. You can also find out what you can do yourself to help preserve the forests on our planet.

Different kinds of forest

The further north you go in the northern hemisphere, the colder it gets and the shorter the summers are. Meanwhile, areas near to the coast get extra rainfall and fog. These variations in the climate affect the types of trees that will grow there.

Woodlands

Woodlands are found in the southern part of the northern hemisphere because the climate is moderate and it rains regularly through the year. Here the deciduous trees have a growing season of between 140 and 200 days, when it is warm enough for them to make the energy they need to get bigger.

As winter approaches the trees store the nutrients from their leaves to use as an energy supply during the winter. The leaves themselves die and fall to the ground.

The quality of the soil is improved by the dead leaves as they gradually rot, which makes the deciduous forest floor a good place for small plants and fungi to grow.

There are several different types of woodland. Some of them have a mixture of broad-leaved and needle-leaved trees growing together in the same wood.

The boreal forest

The boreal forest is named after Boreas, ancient Greek god of the chilly north wind. In boreal forest areas the summer is short and wet. The winters are long, severely cold and dry, and the ground freezes. Because of this the trees have only a short 130-day growing season.

Winters get colder the further north you go in the boreal forest. Winter temperatures

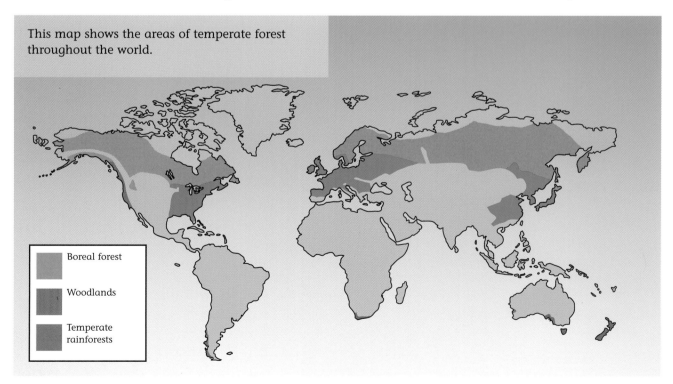

This map shows the areas of temperate forest throughout the world.

Boreal forest

Woodlands

Temperate rainforests

can plunge to -54°C (-65°F), too cold for most creatures to survive. The soil here is poor, so compared to woodlands there are few small plants growing on the forest floor.

In the USA the boreal forest stretches from Alaska all the way down to the Great Lakes, and isolated stretches grow on some high mountains, such as the Appalachians.

Temperate rainforests

Most of the world's rainforests grow in the hot climate around the equator. But along the Pacific northwest coast of the USA there is enough mild weather and moisture for temperate rainforest to grow. The trees here are very ancient and rare, and include Sitka spruces which live for over 1,000 years. There are also areas of temperate rainforest in the southern hemisphere; in Australia, New Zealand, South Africa and Chile in South America.

Unlike the trees in the boreal forest, evergreens can grow all year round in the rainforest because of the mild climate. This allows some species to grow to a huge size.

Epiphytes (plants that grow on other plants) thrive here. They hang down from the tree branches and dangle their roots in the air to get the moisture they need.

The temperate rainforest areas of Australia and New Zealand contain tree and animal species found nowhere else.

Giant redwood trees in the Pacific coast forests of the USA can reach heights of 90 m (300 ft) and up to 30 m (100 ft) around.

How trees work

Trees do things which affect our climate, the land we live on and the air we breathe. Because the northern forests and woodlands are so huge, these processes have a marked effect which scientists can measure.

Photosynthesis

Trees create their own food by a process called photosynthesis. They take in water and a gas called carbon dioxide (CO_2). Then, using sunlight and a green chemical called chlorophyll, the leaves convert the water and CO_2 into sugar and oxygen. The sugar is used as fuel to help the tree grow. The oxygen is expelled into the air.

During the growing season of the huge northern forest regions, there is so much photosynthesis going on that scientists can measure worldwide levels of CO_2 falling, and levels of oxygen rising. If northern forests disappear, that high level of photosynthesis will stop. That could have a drastic effect on the Earth's air and climate.

Carbon dioxide is a gas that is released when fuel such as wood or coal burns. Too much of it in the air leads to global warming – when the Earth's climate gets warmer (see p 18). Oxygen (O_2) is a gas that all life on Earth needs in order to survive. With less photosynthesis we would have more CO_2 and less O_2 in the atmosphere.

Water recycling

Trees are champion water recyclers. When water falls to the ground as rain or snow, the trees take up the water through their roots. It eventually gets recycled back into the air when it evaporates out through the leaves. Finally it falls to Earth again and the process keeps going.

If huge areas of forest disappear, this natural water recycling will decline and there could be an effect on the amount of rain that falls around the world. Farming might suffer, affecting our food supplies.

Soil anchors

Tree roots help to anchor the soil to the ground. This is especially important in the boreal forest where the soil is thin and sandy.

If the boreal forests are destroyed this poor thin soil won't be much good for farming, and it will easily get blown away by the wind.

We can find an example of what might happen by looking back in history. In the 1930s large-scale cutting down of trees helped to cause a "dustbowl" in the US Midwest, making life there very difficult. Terrible duststorms occurred, caused by the wind whipping up the soil.

The secret of leaves

Water is the key to why deciduous trees lose their leaves, but evergreen trees keep their needles.

When cold weather comes to the northern hemisphere, the ground freezes. This makes it

impossible for trees to collect water through their roots. Instead they need to save a store of water inside them until spring.

Broad leaves lose water quickly because it evaporates out of their wide surface. In winter losing so much moisture would mean death for a broad-leafed tree, so it's better for the leaves to die off and then regrow in spring when the ground thaws.

Needle-shaped leaves don't lose anywhere near as much water, because their surface is very small and they have a waxy coating on them. They don't need to die off in winter, and as soon as the sun comes out in spring they can start photosynthesizing straight away. That way evergreen trees get the longest possible growing season, which they need in a region where summers are short.

The leaves of deciduous trees turn beautiful colours before they die and fall off in the autumn.

The life of a tree

Fallen "nurse logs" in a temperate rainforest provide good places for tree seedlings to grow.

Many different types of tree grow in woodlands and forests around the world, but they all have some things in common. They grow leaves, seeds and new wood.

Trees from seeds

A tree begins its life by sprouting from a seed. The seed might be in a nut, a fruit, a cone or perhaps a propeller blown around by the wind. Different tree species make different types of seed.

Boreal trees such as conifers make seeds on the end of scales that are packed together in cones. The cones shed the seeds when they are ripe, which normally takes two or three years. An exception is the ancient sequoia tree of the temperate rainforest. It may keep its cones for up to 20 years before they drop.

Time to sprout

Once a tree seedling sprouts it must try to grow on the forest floor, which is difficult because the large trees overhead block out the light. The best chance is to sprout in a space made by a fallen tree.

In the temperate rainforest, saplings sometimes sprout and grow on "nurse logs". These are fallen trees, which soon start to rot because the atmosphere is so damp. Mosses, lichens and ferns quickly cover the damp log and help to rot it, making it a nutritious place for the seedling to live. Gradually, as the tree grows bigger it throws out roots around the nurse log. Some temperate rainforest trees look like they are standing on stilts because the nurse logs they grew on have long since rotted, leaving a gap between their roots.

In the last decade scientists have begun to study the temperate rainforests of the American northwest in greater detail. They use ropes and harnesses, and even cranes, to climb up into trees as high as skyscrapers. Up in the greenery they have found some surprising new facts about the life of the trees.

When they climbed the big-leaf maples in the Olympic National Park, Washington, they discovered thick bundles of mosses and lichens that gradually rotted to form piles of soil high up in the trees' nooks and crannies. They also found that the trees sent some of their own roots upwards into this soil to collect its nutrients.

Inside a tree

A tree is made up of layers of different cells that do different jobs. A layer called the vascular cambium grows a new section of wood every year, which shows up as a tree ring on cut wood. You can count the rings on a tree log to see how old it is. At the very centre of the tree is its oldest, hardest wood, called the heartwood.

Other layers of tree cells transport water, sap or resin around the tree. Sap is a sugary solution that helps the tree to grow. Maple syrup is made from the delicious sap of northern forest maples.

Resin is made by conifers and some deciduous trees. It is sticky like treacle, and contains powerful chemicals. If the tree gets damaged, the resin oozes out and hardens to heal the wound.

The outer bark is wrapped round the tree to protect it. Some trees, such as the birch, have thin papery bark. Others have thick rough bark. The bark of the giant sequoia is so thick and spongy that it is virtually fireproof, so the tree can survive forest fires.

Tree rings can help scientists work out the weather in the past. Trees grow less in dry years, creating narrowly spaced rings; wide rings show it was wet.

Forest animals

Forests and woodlands are rich in animal life of different kinds. The animals get their food supply from plants or by hunting other creatures. In winter they have different ways of coping with the cold.

Connections of life

The well-being of all the animals and plants in the forest is closely interconnected. The meat-eating carnivores, such as the hawks and the wolves, can only survive by eating smaller animals. Those creatures may, in turn, only survive by eating plants. The plants may only be able to grow because insects help to pollinate them.

If trees die, or water or soil gets polluted, plants and animals can be badly affected and because of all the interconnections between the forest creatures, the death of one plant or animal species can have far-reaching effects. You can find out more about this on page 18.

Mammals

The large forest mammals include herbivores such as the moose and the white-tailed deer, and omnivores such as bears, who will eat both plants and meat. Forest carnivores such as grey wolves, lynx and

Some large mammals, such as this grizzly bear in Alaska, USA, are skilled at catching fish in fast-flowing rivers and streams.

mountain lions hunt other creatures for their food.

Some mammals migrate when winter comes, to find a warmer climate. A few species stay and brave the cold. Others go into a long winter sleep called hibernation, which enables them to survive the harsh weather.

The mammals are among the most endangered creatures in the forest, as their food supply dwindles due to deforestation. Carnivores such as the mountain lion are getting much rarer and also more dangerous. When they can't find food in the forest they sometimes stray into human communities.

Birds

A wide range of birds feeds and nests in forests in spring and summer. The largest examples are the eagles – the bald eagle and the golden eagle.

In autumn many forest birds migrate south to warmer places to find food. The berries, seeds and small creatures they eat aren't available in a harsh winter climate.

Water creatures

The many streams, lakes and bogs make a good home for frogs, salamanders and turtles. The lakes and rivers are rich in fish such as trout, perch, pike and salmon.

Fish don't hibernate in winter. Instead they swim to deep waters, which don't freeze up. Then they slow down their body processes so they can survive with less food during the cold season.

Insects and tiny animals

In spring and summer, forests hum with insects. Clouds of flies and mosquitoes fill the air, providing plenty of meals for birds and small animals.

On the ground, especially in woodlands, there are lots of crawling creatures, such as beetles and earwigs, plus millions of tiny creatures too small to see without a microscope. One handful of woodland soil may contain up to 700 million organisms.

Most insects die in winter, leaving behind eggs that will hatch in spring. Meanwhile, worms survive the cold by burrowing deep down beneath the frozen top layer of the soil.

HIBERNATION

Hibernation means going into a deep sleep. In the northern hemisphere, mammals such as bears, bats and gophers (a North American burrowing animal) do this in November, waking up again around March. First they eat a lot of food, to give themselves a store of fat.

Then they hide somewhere sheltered, such as a cave. As they sleep their body temperature falls, their heartbeat and their breathing slows, and they live off the fat in their bodies. Their bodies are able to "tick over", staying alive but not active.

Natural tree enemies

Trees have some natural enemies that can damage and eventually kill them. However, the worst ones have been acccidentally introduced to forest areas by humans. Scientists have then had to find ways to limit the destruction.

Insect attack

Tree pests include caterpillars that eat leaves and wood-boring beetles that burrow into wood to lay eggs. When the eggs hatch, the larvae eat out tunnels under the bark and eventually chew their way to the surface. Although the insects themselves don't kill the tree, they make openings for fungi to get under the tree bark. Some fungi can stop a tree getting the nutrients and water it needs, eventually killing it altogether.

Normally, tree-attacking insects don't kill whole forests. In fact, they help to get rid of unhealthy or old trees which are more easily attacked. That leaves room for younger, healthier ones to grow. Generally natural pests are part of the balance of nature in a local area, but when humans introduce new pests, devastation can follow.

The chestnut blight disaster

Once 4,000 million majestic chestnut trees covered the eastern USA. They were prized for their wood and their sweet nuts. But in 1904 a deadly fungus called chestnut blight was introduced into the country when some Asian chestnut trees were brought over and cultivated for their larger nuts. The US trees were not naturally immune to the fungus, and over the next few decades 3,500 million chestnut trees died.

Tree scientists had to find some way to stop the devastation. They discovered a harmless form of the fungus that, when injected into a tree, stops the spread of the deadly form. They also started crossing different chestnut tree-types to breed new US chestnut species that were immune to the fungus.

Work on tree and plant diseases is called "plant pathology". Like scientists working in human medicine, plant pathologists try to find out why diseases are occurring and how to cure them.

Dutch Elm devastation

The Dutch Elm fungus probably came originally from the Himalayas in India, on wooden crates made of infected wood. It is passed on by the elm bark beetle. It caused the destruction of millions of elm trees in Europe and the USA during the twentieth century.

Scientists at the University of Toronto studied the problem and found that elms have a natural defence system against disease attack that could be boosted by a tree injection called an "elicitor". The injection helps the tree to grow thicker walls around its cells, keeping out the fungus and preventing its spread.

The wrong wildlife

When new wildlife is introduced to an area by humans, it can have a harmful effect on forests. For instance, when grey squirrels were introduced to British forests from the USA, no-one realized they would be so successful that they would drive out the harmless local red squirrels. Grey squirrels cause lots of damage by eating tree bark, crops and birds.

Nowadays we know a lot more about the potentially disastrous effect of changing a natural environment, and a lot more effort is made to stop non-native animals and plants being spread to new areas where they might cause problems.

This row of elm trees, killed by Dutch Elm fungus, shows the destructive power of blights and diseases.

Acid attack

These trees in the Harz Mountains, Germany, have been badly damaged by acid rain.

In the past century a new danger has begun to threaten the forests. Pollution caused by factories, power plants and car exhausts has produced acid rain, a potential tree killer.

Making acid rain

When fuels such as coal and oil burn they make chemicals that rise up into the air. Two of these chemicals – sulphur dioxide and nitrogen oxide – cause acid rain. Up in the atmosphere they mix with water. Then sunlight helps turn the mixture into sulphuric acid and nitric acid. These harmful substances fall to earth in rain, snow or fog. Acid rain is particularly bad in forests on high mountains which get lots of fog.

Wind can blow the acid pollution far away from the place where it was first made. It may even end up falling in a different country. Some acid rain pollution is made naturally, for instance by erupting volcanoes or forest fires. But most of it is made by industry and by car exhaust fumes.

Not all acid pollution falls as rain. Some of it falls straight to the ground as tiny particles, poisoning the soil. Soil affected in this way has an unusually high amount of metals in it, such as aluminium and lead.

Scientists measure acid and its opposite, alkali, using a pH scale of numbers. The lower the number, the more acid there is. Ordinary rain has a pH of 5.5. Rain below pH 5 is regarded as damaging acid rain.

The effect on forests

Acid rain takes away important minerals from tree leaves and from the soil. It can block up the tiny pores on leaves and stop them from working properly. Meanwhile, the toxic metals it releases into the soil damage a tree's roots. Trees affected this way weaken and stop growing properly. Eventually they might die.

Meanwhile, the acid rain falls into the forest lakes and streams. Animals drink the polluted water or eat the pollution particles and harmful metals begin to build up in their bodies, damaging their health and eventually making them infertile.

Tiny forest plants called lichens are a good indicator of the level of acid rain pollution in an area, because the rain kills them quickly. In a place affected by acid rain, lichens soon disappear.

DEAD LAKES

A forest lake affected by acid rain looks very clear and clean. That's because all the tiny plankton and plants in the water have died. It may look clean, but it is lifeless.

Healthy forest lakes have a pH measurement of about 6.5, and are home to all kinds of creatures and plants. Once the pH drops below 6 everything begins to die out.

In the heavily forested country of Sweden there are about 90,000 lakes and over half of them have been polluted by acid rain. In the USA it's estimated that 1 in 5 lakes has this problem.

Another danger to forest water is effluent: liquid waste pumped into rivers by local industries. Fish stocks such as salmon are badly affected when this happens.

Finding out the facts

Mapping pollution

Around the world there are monitoring stations fitted with equipment to measure acid rain and particle pollution. Filters at the sites gather particles from the air, and the results are checked by chemists. Samples are also gathered from planes sent over forests, and from equipment set up on high forest platforms.

Now pollution is monitored from space, too. Satellites use sensing equipment to collect data on the atmosphere. For instance, satellite sensors can measure the atmosphere for levels of carbon monoxide, a polluting gas produced by cars.

Scientists have developed computer programs that can use all this data to build virtual models of the Earth's atmosphere and landscape. These maps can show where the pollution is coming from and where it is likely to move next.

On the ground, forest experts keep a close eye on the state of trees and take soil, air and water samples to analyse. By studying soil samples scientists have discovered that rich thick soil is much better at coping with acid rain than thin crumbly soil, which is one reason why the effects of pollution vary from place to place.

Animal indicators

Animal experts study forest creatures, recording their population rates, diet and way of life. They have found that when the biggest forest creatures, the carnivores, start dying out, it is often a sign of difficulties all the way down the food chain.

One example of this is the work done on ospreys and bald eagles in the Great Lakes region of North America. Experts discovered that the birds weren't breeding successfully. It turned out that many of their eggshells were so weak that they broke before the chicks could hatch. This was due to the toxic chemicals that had built up in the fish the birds were eating. Some types of agricultural pesticides were pinpointed as a problem, and their use was limited by law.

GLOBAL WARMING

The phrase "global warming" means the warming up of the Earth's atmosphere. Scientific data appears to show it is happening, and it could be due to pollution. The gas CO_2, released when wood, coal or oil burns, is increasing in the atmosphere and could be helping to blanket the Earth so that less heat escapes into space.

The forests use vast amounts of CO_2 in photosynthesis (see p 8), and the trees store huge amounts of carbon in their wood. What would happen if the forests died, ending their photosynthesis and releasing lots of carbon dioxide when they were burnt?

It's still uncertain what the exact effects could be, and the subject causes heated debates between conservationists, industry and even countries around the world.

Since the reduction in use of certain types of agricultural pesticides in the Great Lakes area of North America, the populations of osprey and bald eagle (shown here) have begun to recover.

Fighting back for forests

The middle of a busy city or an industrial factory complex may seem a long way away from a quiet forest glade, but what happens in these highly developed places affects the forests very much because pollution is blown long distances by the wind. Here are a few of the answers scientists have come up with to limit forest damage.

Factory clean-up

Most acid rain gases come from factories, power stations and oil refineries. These gases can be greatly reduced by fitting new equipment that limits gas emissions. For instance, sulphur gas can be absorbed as it goes up a factory chimney.

Pulp and paper mills are often found in forest areas. Once fitted with treatment machinery, their liquid waste (called effluent) can be made non-toxic before it is washed into nearby rivers.

Industrial clean-up inventions have led to a drop in pollution in many areas in the last few years. But it adds cost to businesses, so not all companies around the world are happy to do it.

Factories and power stations, such as this one near Hong Kong, can be fitted with equipment to help reduce the amount of pollution they make.

LAND OF THE SPOTTED OWL

The northern spotted owl lives in areas of "old-growth" conifer forest in the Pacific northwest of the USA. "Old-growth" means forest that has never been cut down and replanted. In the early 1990s logging was halted in 17 US National Forest Parks to protect the owl.

Conservationists were delighted but loggers were furious. They couldn't agree which was more important – protecting creatures or making an income from jobs. Conservationists argue that we must try to keep "biodiversity", which means preserving as many animal and plant species as possible to try to keep the Earth healthy. They argue it's impossible to put a price on that.

Either way, conservation measures are still a hot political issue in many countries.

Cleaning up cars

Car exhaust fumes are full of poisonous gases. New cars are now fitted with a catalytic converter, a chamber in the exhaust system that alters the gases and makes them much less harmful.

One day non-polluting electric cars may become more popular. Scientists have even invented solar cars that are powered by sunlight, and cars powered by non-polluting vegetable oil.

Changing laws

Acid rain pollution is an issue for the whole world, because one country's industrial pollution can harm another country's forest.

International laws have been passed to try to limit poisonous gas pollution. But some countries refuse to sign up because they think it might damage the profits of their industries, and cost jobs.

Saving lakes

Acidity in lakes can be controlled by adding lots of lime to the water. Lime is a harmless alkaline, the opposite type of substance to acid. It can be pumped into a river or lake, but its effects don't last forever. It has to be added again every few years to help the water support life.

Increased car usage leads to more acid rain.

Using forests

Wood from forests is used in many different ways in our homes, and in industry, too. Electricity can come from forest hydro-electric schemes, and some forest areas have oil resources. The effect of all this industry on forests and on local people is very controversial. Businesses, governments and conservationists argue bitterly over it.

Forest industry

Forest products include furniture, building materials of all kinds, paper and fuel logs.

Industrial timber companies practise "clear-cutting", which means cutting down wide areas of forest in one go. The timber companies are encouraged to replant the trees. This is called "sustainable" forestry, and in places such as North America and Northern Europe it is increasing.

In more faraway isolated places, such as the Russian taiga, conservationists fear unscrupulous companies could do great damage by clear-cutting vast areas without replanting.

Some would prefer to preserve the wilderness untouched, but in the meantime the world demand for wood is rocketing, so conservationists and businesses are trying to work together to regenerate the forest. The best forest businesses do all they can to renew the forest they use, recycle their waste and make sure they aren't polluting the local water supply. But this does not happen all over the world.

A "clear-cut" area, where all the trees have been cut down.

FIRST NATIONS

Although the boreal forest has a low population, many of its people have a long history and a unique culture. In Canada there are many First Nations reservations in forested areas. The people of these tribes traditionally rely on the forest to make a living, doing their own logging and wood product-making. They battle to save their forest from large-scale industrial damage and pollution. Without the forest, they know their way of life would disappear.

In Europe the Sami people in northern Scandinavia make their living from herding reindeer, but their rights to herd through the boreal forest are being challenged by private forest owners.

Meanwhile in the far eastern area of Russia, ancient tribes such as the Koryak people are fast disappearing as their way of life dies out. They have found they have no rights over the forest their ancestors once cared for.

Problems with plantations

Sometimes "old-growth" forest, usually a mix of different trees, gets cut down and replanted as a commercial plantation with only one fast-growing conifer tree species in it. When that happens a lot of the original wildlife and plants disappear forever. Conifer plantations with just one type of tree support far fewer plants and animals than a mix of trees. Conservationists encourage companies to replant using a mix, to try to help preserve wildlife.

Non-wood industries

The industries that most damage the forest are the ones that do not replace the trees they clear. Oil extraction, mining, road-building, hydro-electric dams, the building of new communities and the use of land for farming all destroy trees forever. If planned badly they can cause serious damage and pollution of the water supplies in the local area. But, on the other hand, these activities bring jobs and money to northern forest countries.

Logging brings jobs and money to forest areas.

Managing a forest

Foresters try to look after forested areas so that they stay healthy and productive. The science of managing a woodland is called silviculture.

When to cut
A forest that is overcrowded can start to get unhealthy. Foresters need to cut down diseased trees to stop problems spreading, and they sometimes need to thin out forests, cutting down some of the tallest oldest trees to give the younger shorter trees more light to help them grow.

Many birds, such as these woodpeckers, eat forest insects, including harmful pests.

However, it is a good idea to leave a few dead tree skeletons in a forest. They are called snags and they make good nesting homes for useful birds such as woodpeckers, which help keep the forest healthy by eating insect pests.

Clear-cutting properly
Clear-cutting means cutting down all the trees in an area. Large ill-planned clear-cutting can lead to soil being eroded, local water supplies being polluted and wildlife being destroyed. Carefully planned clear-cutting can avoid the problems. For instance, strips of untouched forest called buffer strips can be left between clear-cuts to encourage wildlife and protect streams.

Clear-cutting leaves a landscape looking bare and scarred, but the forest will gradually regrow through natural seeding and replanting. It takes about twenty years for a clear-cut forest to regenerate completely.

Forest fire
For many years in the forests of the USA all forest fires were put out. Gradually the forest undergrowth grew thicker and the trees got overcrowded. Eventually this caused fire to rage much more uncontrollably whenever it did accidentally break out.

Now it's understood that carefully controlled fire is good for forests. It helps to clear out dead undergrowth and it even helps some seeds to grow. Nowadays foresters are allowed to start fires deliberately in forests that need clearing. But first they chemically treat undergrowth and dig ditches around the planned fire area. The ditches stop the fire from spreading, and the treatment of the undergrowth helps prevent the fire from flaring up too much.

Unplanned forest fires can be started by lightning strikes, or by careless human behaviour such as lighting campfires during a spell of dry weather. When accidental fires threaten human safety, teams of firefighters sometimes go into the fire area by helicopter. Highly trained firefighters called "smoke-jumpers" parachute down to try to stop the fire spreading. Planes may also be sent in to bomb the fire with water.

Forests make money

People love to visit forests. In fact forest tourism makes much more money than timber-logging. For instance, millions of people visit the National Forest Parks in the USA every year and generate $100,000 million for the US economy.

Forest managers must plan paths for the visitors, safely away from dangers such as rockfalls or breeding wild bears. Visitors need facilities such as parking places, campsites and information centres where they can learn about the forest and the creatures that live there.

People love to go for walks through woodlands. Clearly marked paths help protect fragile plants.

Watching the forest

It's important for scientists to study and map the world's forests. That way it's easier to keep track of dangers, such as fires, the effects of pollution and illegal logging, and also to work out how best to keep this vast area of the Earth healthy.

Mapping with satellites

Mapping remote areas of forest has been made easier by GPS (Global Positioning System). GPS consists of 27 satellites orbiting the Earth. At any time, anywhere on the Earth, someone with a GPS receiver can locate four of these satellites. The receiver measures its distance from each satellite and uses the data to work out its own position on the ground.

In a remote forest, GPS is vital for finding your way around and for recording the position of geographical features such as hills and rivers.

Computer pictures

Forest-watching is made a lot easier by computers, which can store all kinds of data and convert it into 3D pictures.

A computer GIS (Geographical Information System) can be used to create a range of 3D maps, for instance showing different kinds of trees, forest fires and burnt areas,

This satellite image shows a forest fire in progress in Montana, USA.

places where erosion is happening or local streams and rivers.

Programs of this kind can even be made to predict future events, using the data they have to create maps of what is likely to happen. They might be used to predict forest growth, soil erosion or flooding.

Watching from above

Sensors on planes and satellites can be used to build up pictures of the land down below. For instance, airborne radar can be used to plot the shape of the land, and a satellite image can show different forest features in lots of detail. It might show up an area where trees are being cut down illegally.

Predicting fires

Forest experts try to predict forest fires by measuring the moisture in the ground and in firewood logs. If there is lots of moisture there is less likelihood of fire. In times of drought, moisture dries out and fire gets much more likely.

The greenness of a forest is an indicator of fire risk. Once forests start to dry out they lose their greenness.

Up a tree: a scientist captures insects in a net to study later in a laboratory.

KEEPING WATCH ON CRITTERS

Forest biologists study insect wildlife in a forest by climbing the trees and using nets to trap specimens. Back on the ground they take a look at what they've caught. Using this method, hundreds of new insect species have been discovered. By recording them and keeping an eye on whether their numbers rise or fall, biologists may get an early warning if problems begin to hit forest health, for example in the case of an insect-borne blight or disease such as Dutch Elm fungus.

What can you do?

Here are some suggestions for ways that you can find out more about forests and help to stop their destruction.

Watch what you buy

Whenever possible, try to encourage your family to buy wood that has been cut from a sustainable forest that is properly managed to preserve and renew the environment. This type of wood has a forest certificate mark on its packaging, which means the forest it has come from has been independently checked for good forestry. By supporting good forestry you will be helping to maintain both forest communities and the environment.

Recycle your stuff

Try to use recycled paper when you can, and make sure you recycle the paper that you no longer need. In the long run it will help to reduce the number of trees cut down. Find out about recycling schemes in your area, and join in.

Be energy-efficient

Make sure you don't waste energy such as electricity. The less power you use, the less you contribute to global warming.

You can also help by cutting out non-essential car rides. Maybe you could start a car-sharing scheme with your friends when you go to school or on trips.

Be a good visitor

When you visit woodlands or forests, make sure you don't damage plants and wildlife or do something that might start a fire.

If you go to woodlands or forests for a picnic, make sure you take away your rubbish afterwards.

Adopt a tree

All over the world there are adopt-a-tree schemes that you can join to help fund conservation work. Ask your teacher to help you find one near where you live. You can adopt trees for other people, too. This makes an unusual present.

Get involved

Find out if there are schemes you can get involved with to help look after and monitor your local woods. Ask your teacher if you could research ways your class could contribute.

On the Web

Here are some useful website addresses relating to woodlands and forests:

www.nationalgeographic.com
Find out about world habitats, play games and try activities.

www.mobot.org
Find out what it's like to live in deciduous and boreal northern forests in this site run by the Missouri Botanical Gardens.

www.borealforest.org
Find out about the world of boreal forests through this site based on the forests of Northwest Canada.

www.panda.org
Find out about the Worldwide Fund for Nature and its conservation work around the world, including work on the northern forests.

www.familyfun.go.com
Here are some practical fun ideas for things to do next time you visit a woodland. Try working out the age of a tree and even listening to it! Type the word "woods" into the site search section to find a list of ideas.

www.yahooligans.yahoo.com
Once you get on this site go to "science and nature", then to "living things", then to "botany" and finally "trees" to get a long list of tree-related user-friendly sites to explore.

www.futureforests.com
Find out how you can help in the fight against global warming, and dedicate your own baby trees in forests supported by celebrity pop-stars.

www.tappi.org/paperu
Go to "paper university" to find out how paper products are made from wood and to play paper-related games.

Glossary

Acid rain
Moisture containing harmful acid substances. It can fall to Earth as rain, snow or fog.

Bark
A tree's outer protective layer.

Biodiversity
The wide variety of living things on the Earth.

Biome
A continuous stretch of natural area.

Boreal forest
The giant evergreen forest in the upper part of the northern hemisphere.

Broad-leaved trees
Trees with flat wide leaves.

Carbon dioxide (CO²)
A gas released when wood, coal or oil burns.

Carnivores
Animals that only eat meat.

Catalytic converter
Equipment fitted into the exhaust system of a car to make its exhaust less polluting.

Chlorophyll
A green chemical found in plant leaves.

Clear-cutting
Cutting down all the trees in an area.

Cone
The scaly fruit of a pine or fir tree. On the end of each scale is a seed.

Deciduous trees
Trees that lose their leaves in winter.

Deforestation
The destruction of trees over large areas.

Epiphytes
Plants that grow on other plants and dangle their roots in the air to get the moisture they need.

Erosion
When landscape such as soil gets worn away, perhaps by wind or by flooding.

Evergreen trees
Trees that do not lose their leaves in winter.

First Nations
Communities who have lived in the boreal forest for many centuries.

Fungi
Small plants that do not photosynthesize, but instead get the food they need from dead leaves and rotting bark.

GIS
Geographical Information System; a computer program for creating 3D maps.

Heartwood
The oldest hardest layer of wood, found in the centre of a tree.

Herbivores
Animals that only eat plants.

Hibernation
When animals sleep through the winter.

Lichens
Tiny plants that grow on bark or stone.

Migration
When animals travel to new areas to find food. Many northern forest animals migrate south in winter.

Needle-leaved trees
Trees with leaves shaped like tiny needles.

Northern hemisphere
The northern half of the world.

Nurse log
A fallen log that provides an ideal place for a new tree seedling to grow.

Old-growth forest
A forest that has never been harvested and then regrown.

Omnivores
Animals that eat meat and plants.

Oxygen (O₂)
A gas made by trees during photosynthesis.

pH scale
A way to measure the amount of acid in a liquid such as acid rain or forest lakes.

Photosynthesis
The process by which green plants take in sunlight, CO_2 and water to make oxygen and food.

Plant pathology
The study of tree and plant diseases.

Resin
A sticky substance made by a tree to help heal damage to its bark.

Sap
A sugary solution that a tree makes and uses to help it grow.

Silviculture
The science of managing a forest to keep it healthy.

Smoke-jumpers
Highly trained forest firefighters who parachute into threatened forest areas to try to stop fire spreading.

Snag
A dead tree skeleton, still standing in a forest.

Sustainable forestry
Forests that are replanted and managed properly to ensure they regrow after cutting.

Taiga
The name given to the huge area of boreal forest that grows in Russia.

Temperate climate
The mild wet weather in the southern part of the northern hemisphere.

Temperate rainforest
A rainforest that grows in a part of the world where there are cool seasons as well as warm ones.

Tree ring
The new layer of wood that grows each year inside a tree.

Index